"Adult Coloring Delights"
Mythical Creatures and Animal Designs
For Stress Relief

By: Jane Fairley

Our team at "Coloring Delights" brings to you over thirty- two detailed and full page designs to let you escape to a mythical world of the Phoenix, Fairies, Dragons, Centaur, Pegasus, Chimera, Griffin, Unicorn , Mermaid, and many more. Designs are inspired by zentangle method and have beautiful patterns with dazzling background of varieties of flowers, landscape and leaves. Designs are done full page with only one side printed.

Scenes include detailed full body designs of the phoenix bird, a dragon and a beautiful princess, mermaid with an underwater background, a beautiful fairy high up on the trees, Pegasus with a beautiful princess, a full body detailed design of a mythical creature Chimera, a full body design of a woman centaur, a full body design of the mythical bird Griffin with an octopus and many more. Go ahead, and Color yourself away to the mythical world.

Tips before you start to color

1)   Place a loose sheet under your image before you color to protect it from bleeding through to the next page and ruining it.

2)   Who says you need to color the leaves only in green color, there is no proper way to color, just be creative and indulge yourself.

3)   Reduce noise and any distractions before you color to achieve mindfulness and get the right benefits of coloring.

4)   Color yourself away to the mythical world.

For Color Test